300 [...] & Tricks for Guitar

A practical guide for every guitarist.

- **Valuable hints and ideas**
- **Choosing an instrument**
- **Reading music**
- **Chords and scales**
- **Blues, rock, jazz, country, and funk riffs**
- **and much, much more.**

Amsco Publications
New York/London/Sydney

Gibson Explorer owned by Scott Arch
Photographed by William H. Draffen
Project editor: Ed Lozano
Interior design and layout: Len Vogler

Order No. AM 945220
US International Standard Book Number: 0.8256.1632.8
UK International Standard Book Number: 0.7119.6743.1

Exclusive Distributors:
Music Sales Corporation
257 Park Avenue South, New York, NY 10010 USA
Music Sales Limited
8/9 Frith Street, London W1V 5TZ England
Music Sales Pty. Limited
120 Rothschild Street, Rosebery, Sydney, NSW 2018, Australia

Printed in the United States of America by
Vicks Lithograph and Printing Corporation

Contents

Guitar Basics

Buying an Instrument

Many of the basic 'rules' of buying an instrument pertain to both ends of the market although some are aimed exclusively at the inexperienced player:

1 You must be careful that you're buying an instrument that is meant to cater for the style of music you're playing. If you're really obsessed with heavy metal guitar playing, I can't imagine you're going to get the sounds you crave from a classical guitar.

2 Watch out for any instrument with rough fret edges.

3 Don't be bullied into buying something —the salesman may know just as little as you do.

4 As a general guideline, an expensive new item by a major name manufacturer will hold its value much better than a similar priced product from a little known company. You may unexpectedly find a need to sell it for one reason or another, who knows.

5 Find out what are considered to be the best combinations of gear. For instance, my Fender Telecaster sounds amazing through a Fender Twin Reverb but I can't get the type of jazz sound I want from the same amp with an Ibanez Artist guitar.

6 You may have to tailor the kind of amp you use not only to the type of sound you want but also to the type of venues you play. A Marshall stack sounds great at high volume but it's no good to you in a jazz wine bar duo.

7 If you live in a house where practicing is not possible, or if your only practice time comes when respectable people are asleep, you could try using a headphone amp.

8 With headphone amps and beginner level practice amps I would suggest that, if you can afford to, you should buy one with reverb, delay or even chorus. The sound of a cheap amp with nothing to smooth out the tone can be pretty unforgiving.

Tuning

9 The guitar can be tuned with the aid of pitch pipes or dedicated electronic guitar tuners which are available through your local music dealer.

If you do not have a tuning device, you can use relative tuning.

Press down where indicated, one at a time, following the instructions.

Estimate the pitch of the 6th string as near as possible to E or at least a comfortable pitch (not too high, as you might break other strings in tuning up).

Then, while checking the various positions on the diagram, place a finger from your left hand on the:

5th fret of the E or 6th string and tune the open A (or 5th string) to the note A.

5th fret of the A or 5th string and tune the open D (or 4th string) to the note D.

5th fret of the D or 4th string and tune the open G (or 3rd string) to the note G.

4th fret of the G or 3rd string and tune the open B (or 2nd string) to the note B.

5th fret of the B or 2nd string and tune the open E (or 1st string) to the note E.

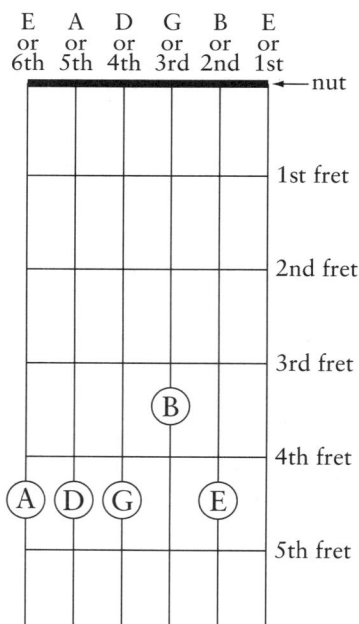

Your Instrument and Accessories

10 If you have to replace any fuses in your gear, always keep some spares at hand. If the fuse blew once, chances are it will happen again.

11 Always carry spare strings—the rest of the band will never forgive you if a string breaks and you can't continue the gig.

12 When re-stringing your guitar, wind the string through the hole and turn the peg so that the string passes over the hole.

13 When the string winds through again make sure it passes under the level of the hole. This puts pressure on the string to stay in place.

14 If the guitar's jack socket comes loose, don't just tighten it up—you'll pull the wires out inside. Instead, hold the socket in place by putting a thin nosed pair of pliers into it, while tightening the nut with your other hand.

15 Tuck your cable over the strap so that the weight of the guitar holds it in place. This means you won't pull the cable out if you step on it.

16 Raise your speakers up off the floor—you'll damp a lot of their projection by putting them on the ground. Also, by raising them higher to your head you'll be able to hear yourself more easily without having to turn the level up.

17 If it's at all possible, refrain from leaving your guitar in a very dry or very hot room. When the moisture leaves the I wood it will contract. This will result in bowing of the neck. Acoustic guitars are particularly prone to cracking due to extreme humidity/temperature changes.

18 If you're traveling, it's possible to buy a humidifier which can be left inside your case or even inside your guitar.

19 Every now and again check the main connections to your equipment to ensure the wiring and fuses are secure.

At Rehearsals/Gigs

20 If you're stacking equipment in a car or van, pack speaker cabinets face down on a flat surface—this will prevent any damage to the grill or speakers.

21 Never leave any of your gear in any vehicle—the chances, of it getting stolen are too great to risk. Also you might find even if the insurance company pays up, you can't really replace that old guitar you've had for years.

22 Don't leave drinks on top of your amplifier—it's an accident waiting to happen.

23 Don't leave your guitar leaning against a chair. If you're not using it either put it on a guitar stand or back in the case.

24 Most guitars these days (except classical guitars) come equipped with a truss rod. This is a strong metal bar running through the neck of the instrument. It is slightly curved and when turned it adjusts the curvature of the neck. You'll need an Allen key to adjust this. The truss rod is generally found under a badge near the nut. If your strings are buzzing in one particular place on the neck of the instrument, you may find a truss rod adjustment will sort it out. Adjust the truss rod in increments of ¼ of a turn.

25 If there's a local music shop with a reputable repairman it's definitely worth getting your guitar 'set up'. This means the height of the strings and the curvature of the neck. The height of the pickups will be (hopefully) adjusted to suit your style of playing.

Effects Units

26 When using effects units, pedals or rack mounted, you'll find the best way to use them is to plug them into your amplifier's send and return sockets. Certain units like the Alesis Quadraverb (great unit that it is!) have a very low output signal if you plug directly through it.

27 You'll find it's worth getting short cables to connect the units in your rack. If you use standard length cables you're likely to get everything into a horrible tangle.

28 Read the manual when you get a new effects box—you'll only get the best out of a unit when you understand how it works.

29 When it comes to buying an effects unit, it's worth thinking about the way you approach learning about such devices. If you're the sort of person who likes to just plug in, dial up a sound and play, then certain of the more modern devices may demand more effort than you're prepared to put in. A simpler device might be sufficient for your needs.

30 When you're setting up your effects units make sure the actual volume is fairly balanced between clean and distorted sounds. This may entail lowering the volume on your distortion unit.

31 If you do use a volume pedal you might try putting it between your pre-amp (if you use one) and power amp. This way you won't lose any of the quality or gain of the pre-amp's tone. This is especially relevant to distorted sounds.

32 If you normally use a lot of delay or reverb it's probably worth creating an effects setting which has just a dry signal in case the band comes to a dead stop. It sounds pretty silly when they've stopped and your note is still ringing.

Safety Precautions

33 Buy a circuit breaker to put between you and your electrical equipment. If you get a shock the power will cut out immediately.

34 Don't fool around with any of your electrical gear while it's plugged in.

35 If you're fitting a plug to a piece of electrical equipment make sure you strip the individual wires just enough to make a connection. You don't want to risk two wires touching if a cable gets tugged.

Reading Music

36 Musical notes are written on a system of five equally spaced horizontal lines called a *staff*. Their position on the staff denotes their pitch.

37 The higher pitched notes (normally played by the right hand on a keyboard instrument) are written in the *treble clef,* the sign for which appears at the beginning of the staff like this:

38 The *bass clef* is used for the lower pitched (left hand) notes and looks like this:

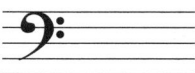

39 Notes are given letter names corresponding to the first seven letters of the alphabet, A to G. This sequence keeps repeating throughout the whole pitch range.

A B C D E F G, A B C D E F G, A B C etc.

40 A note is written either on a *line* or in the *space* between two lines of the staff. The notes on the lines of the treble clef are:

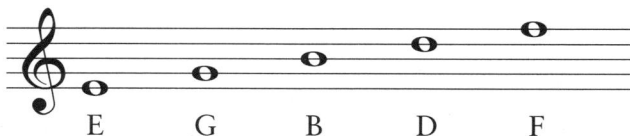

E   G   B   D   F

41 and the notes in the spaces are:

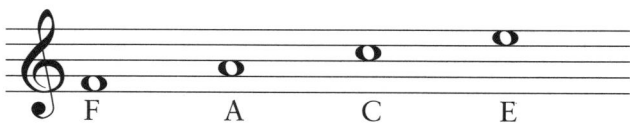

F   A   C   E

42 The notes on the lines of the bass clef are:

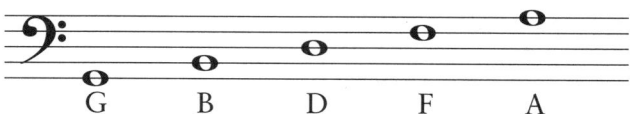

G   B   D   F   A

43 and the notes in the spaces are:

A   C   E   G

44 Note which are too high or too low to be placed on the staff are written on short added lines called *leger lines*, which effectively extend the staff upwards or downwards at that point.

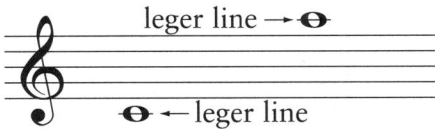

45 This tip shows the most commonly used notes, with their letter names, written in the treble and bass clefs. The note C which is written on a leger line either just below the treble clef or just above the bass clef is called *middle C,* and is found in the middle of the piano keyboard.

46 Each note in a piece of music has a specific length or duration in relation to the other notes. The relative duration is indicated by the appearance of the note. Each type of note also has a corresponding symbol called a *rest*, which indicates a period of silence of equal duration. Here are some of the most common notes and their rests, starting with the longest.

47 A *whole note*

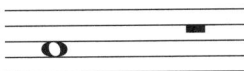

lasts twice as long as:

48 A *half note*

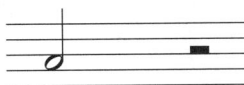

which lasts twice as long as:

49 A *quarter note*

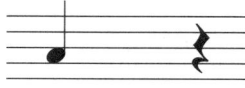

which lasts twice as long as:
50 An *eighth note*

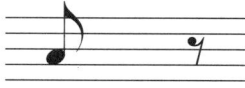

which lasts twice as long as:
51 A *sixteenth note*.

52 Pairs of eighth notes are often joined by a horizontal line called a *beam*, and similarly groups of four sixteenth notes may be joined by a double beam:

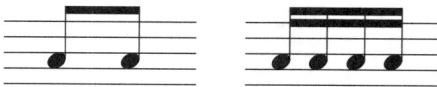

53 Most music has a regular pulse or *beat*. It is divided by *barlines* into short sections of equal duration called *measures* (or *bars*), and each bar in a piece usually contains the same number of beats. Two numbers placed one above the other just after the clef sign at the beginning of the piece comprise the *time signature*. The upper number gives the number of beats in a bar and the lower number shows the value for one beat.

54 In the following example there are three beats in the measure, and each beat is a quarter note. (The number 4 indicates quarter notes; if the number were 8 then each beat would be an eighth note.)

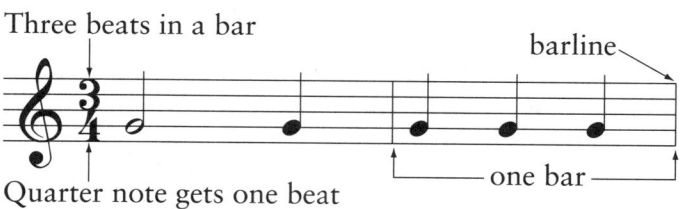

Three beats in a bar

barline

Quarter note gets one beat

one bar

55 When a dot is placed after a note it increases its length by half as much again.

tie

=

56 In the previous example the curved line joining the two notes of the same pitch is called a *tie,* and means that the first note is held on for the length of both notes added together without the second one being played. But a curved line joining two or more notes of different pitch is called a *slur,* and means that the notes are to be played smoothly, without any gaps between them.

slur

57 A *double barline* (often called simply a double bar) is used to show the end of a section in a piece of music:

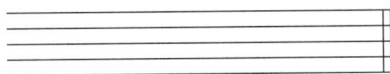

58 At the end of a piece the second bar line is thicker for greater emphasis:

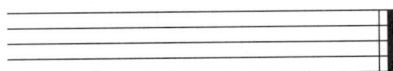

59 If a section of music is to be played twice, it need only be written out once and *repeat signs* placed at the beginning and end of it:

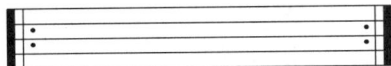

60 Sometimes a repeated section has a different ending. In this case the *1st and 2nd ending bars* are used to accommodate the differences.

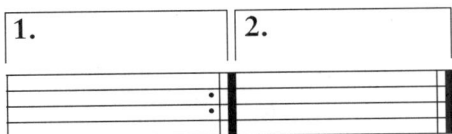

1.

2.

Scales and Keys

61 The pitch distance between a note and the next nearest note is called a *half-step.* The distance between a note and the next note a *whole-step* (two half-steps). There are two main types of scales in Western music, *Major* and *Minor.* The scale of C major is shown here. All the notes in the scale are a whole-step apart, except for E-F and B-C (marked with slurs).

= whole step
= half step

62 When scales start on notes other than C the same sequence of tones and half-steps still has to be maintained. To do this some notes have to be altered (raised or lowered) by using *sharps* or *flats*. The following signs can be placed in front of the note.

63 A sharp ♯ raises the note a half-step.

64 A flat ♭ lowers the note a half-step.

65 A natural sign ♮ cancels the effect of a previous sharp or flat.

66 A double sharp ✗ raises a note a tone (two half-steps).

67 A double flat ♭♭ lowers a note a tone (two half-steps).

68 *Key signatures* are used at the beginning of each staff to show which key a piece is in, and also to permanently raise or lower the pitch of certain notes to maintain the correct sequence of whole- and half-steps in the scale. Minor scales use a different sequence of whole- and half-steps from major. Here is a scale of A minor (melodic form). The sequence of whole- and half-steps varies depending on whether the scale is ascending or descending.

69 The key signatures of all the major and minor keys are shown below:

F♯ major or
D♯ minor

G♭ major or
E♭ minor

C♯ major or
A♯ minor

C♭ major or
A♭ minor

70 *Compound time* is where the basic pulse of the music is subdivided into uneven groups of beats. For instance, ⁶₈ the bars are divided into two groups of three eighth notes.

71 The ¹²₈ time signature is frequently used in guitar music, especially the blues. Here the bars are subdivided into four groups of three eighth notes each.

72 At moderate tempos in blues music, ¹²₈ has many similarities with ⁴₄. It's just that the beats have more of a bouncy feel in ¹²₈.

73 Musical notation can convey more than just the notes—observe indications as to dynamics, phrasing and form.

74 Guitar chords are displayed as diagrams that represent the fingerboard of the guitar. There are six vertical lines representing the six strings of the guitar. Horizontal lines represent the frets. The strings are arranged with the high E (first, or thinnest) string to the right, and the low E (sixth, or thickest) to the left. The black circles indicate at which fret the finger is to be placed and the number tells you which finger to use. At the top of the diagram there is a thick black line indicating the nut of the guitar. Diagrams for chords up the neck just have a fret line at the top with a Roman numeral to the right to identify the first fret of the diagram. You will occasionally see Xs and Os. An X indicates that the string below it is either not played or damped, an O simply means the string is played as an open string.

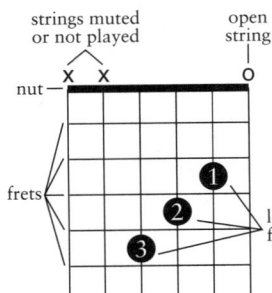

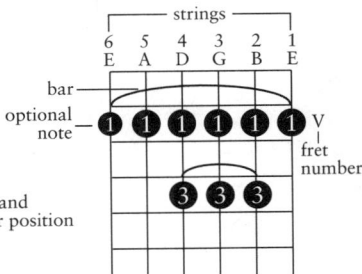

strings muted or not played
open string
— strings —
6 5 4 3 2 1
E A D G B E
nut
bar
optional note
V
fret number
frets
left hand finger position

75 If a piece is a 'swing' tune this means there's a lilt to the eighth notes. In fact, where you see:

┌─ 3 ─┐

you should play these notes as:

76 If you see this symbol ✗ you are instructed to repeat the previous bar. This device saves copyists and composers a good deal of time. It also means your brain isn't analyzing the same bar over and over again.

77 The term 'comping' means accompaniment. It's most frequently used in jazz contexts.

78 The symbol for a downstroke of the pick is: ⊓

79 The symbol for an upstroke of the pick is: V

80 The symbol for a major 7 chord is: maj7

81 The symbol for a minor 7 chord is: m7

82 The symbol for a diminished chord is: ° or dim

83 The symbol for an augmented chord is: + or aug

84 Classical guitar notation gives names to the right hand fingers. The thumb is notated by the symbol *p*, the index finger by *i*, the second finger by *m*, the ring finger by *a* and the rarely used little finger by *c*.

Movement and Improvement

85 It is very important to realize the need for good posture when you play. Over time, bad posture will inhibit your progress and could eventually lead to fairly serious physical problems .

86 Whichever style of music you're playing try not to allow yourself to slouch or bend your body too far around the instrument.

87 Classical guitar players favor the use of a footrest to support the left leg, thereby raising the instrument higher up the torso and facilitating better access to the instrument. If you're a fingerstyle player (non-classical), it might be worth checking out if a footrest might help your posture.

88 If you do gigs standing up, make sure that you spend at least some of your practice time standing up. You use the muscles in your arms, back and shoulders in a different way when sitting.

89 Be careful with the length of your strap——if it's hanging down by your knees it might look cool but you're not going to have the best access to the notes. It's a question of fashion versus command of the instrument.

Technique—Left Hand

90 Develop your left hand so that you're only using the weight of the finger to fret the note—any more pressure is merely a waste of effort and inhibits flexibility.

91 The left-hand thumb is strongest when placed in the middle of the neck of the guitar, just opposite the second left-hand finger.

92 If you suffer from tension in your fingers, then you're obviously overpressing. Spend some time each day experimenting with the minimum amount of finger pressure. The aim is to educate your fingers to accept the fact that their weight alone is sufficient to make any note/chord sound.

93 Even if you're not particularly feeling tension in your hands and arms it's a good idea to get up out of your seat every twenty minutes. Move around and stretch your arms.

94 *Bar chord*—where the left hand index finger is flattened on the fingerboard to hold down more than one note. E.g.:

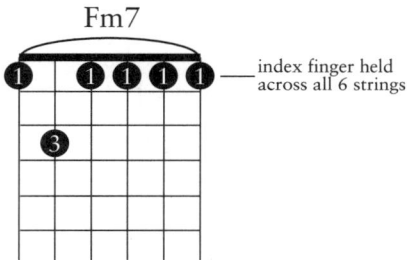

95 Practice bending in tune. Try this exercise.

96 Now this:

97 Now this:

Right-Hand Picking Techiques

98 Hammerons.

* Continue across all six strings

99 Pulloffs.

100

101 Various combinations of hammerons and pulloffs.

102

103

104

105

106

107

108

109

110

111 'Alternate picking' is probably the most obvious way of plucking the strings—you just alternate between downstrokes ⊓ and upstrokes ∨.

112 Some players almost exclusively use downstrokes. As with anything else to do with technique, if it works why change it?

113 Note that the faster you play, the smaller your right hand movements must become. Very fast articulation requires that you make only very small movements.

114 If you play fingerstyle you'll have to spend a little time playing exercises which alternate adjacent right-hand fingers. With a little practice you'll be able to liberate them from one another. If you're just starting out you'll probably have to decide whether to base your technique on the pick or the use of your right-hand fingers. If you play classical guitar you'll definitely have to use your fingers. However, in most other styles there is generally room for both approaches.

115 If you normally use a pick but need to play arpeggio-type patterns, you'll find it's pretty tricky playing these types of figures with a pick. Why don't you try holding the pick normally but also use the 2nd, 3rd, and even the 4th right hand fingers to pick out the notes on the higher strings.

116 You will occasionally drop a pick. If you're doing a gig, you might try attaching a few picks to a microphone stand with adhesive tape.

Right-Hand Tapping

117 Right-hand tapping is a technique where the right-hand fingers are used to execute hammer-ons and pulloffs. The main benefit of this technique is that slurs can be executed beyond the reach of the left hand. To start tapping use only the right index or second finger.

118 (T= tap or hammer-on with your right hand)

119

120 This line includes a slide executed by the right-hand tapping finger.

121

Classical Guitars—
Specific Right-Hand Techniques

122 *Tremolo* is a technique where a melodic line (generally quite a slow moving one) is played in quick repeated notes to create a shimmering sort of effect. The thumb generally picks out a bass note (but sometimes hits the repeated melody note) while in turn the ring, second and index fingers pick out the repeated top note.

123

124

125

Care of the Hands

126 Keep the fingernails of your left hand quite short— the most accurate way of fretting a note is with the tip of the finger. It's pretty painful if you trap a string under a fingernail.

127 Classical/fingerstyle players must keep their right hand nails well filed. The nail has a grain, just like a piece of wood—a tear on the edge of the nail will easily spread down the grain.

128 To maintain a smooth edge you will need a nail file and some fine emery or sand paper (buy the finest grade possible).

129 If you have particularly weak nails you can use false nails as a substitute or strengthen your own by applying a layer of clear nail varnish.

Tunings

130 Apart from the standard tuning there are a number of other tunings which have been commonly used. Blues players are the most adventurous group where tunings are concerned.

131 Open E tuning
1=E, 2=B, 3=G♯, 4=E, 5=B, 6=E

132 Open D tuning
l=D, 2=A, 3=F♯, 4=D, 5=A, 6=D

133 Open G tuning
l=D, 2=B, 3=G, 4=D, 5=G, 6=D

134 Try tuning your guitar a half-step flat
l=E♭, 2=B♭, 3=G♭, 4=D♭, 5=A♭, 6=E♭

135 Try tuning your guitar a tone flat
1=D, 2=A, 3=F, 4=C, 5=G, 6=D
Tips 134 and 135 give a fatter, looser sort of sound.

136 If you're using one of the last two tunings, you may find it necessary to use a heavier gauge of string to preserve the feel of the strings (and to enhance the tone).

137 One tuning which is very popular with folk guitarists is:
1=D, 2=A, 3=G, 4=D, 5=A, 6=D

Tricks and Devices

138 If you're the sort of player who uses a lot of open position chords, you should get yourself a capo. This is a metal clamp which depresses all the strings in one fret space. It's particularly useful for accompanists where the singer wants to perform in a key for which open position chords

139 To give a smooth start to a note or chord, try fading in with a volume pedal or by rolling the volume control on your instrument—this is a useful device to give contrast it makes the instrument sound less guitar-like and percussive in attack.

140 Artificial harmonics can be achieved by fretting a note normally with the left hand then lightly touching the string, twelve, seven or five frets higher with the right-hand index finger. The third right-hand finger is then used to pluck the string.

141 Artificial harmonics can also be played when you fret a note normally with the left hand but lightly touch the string with the flesh of your right hand while picking with a pick.

142 Use this technique when you haven't got the time to put the pick down to play an artificial harmonic.

143 Note that some artificial harmonics don't sound fully when certain pick-ups are used. This is because the magnetic pull of a pick-up will suppress the vibration of the string on various notes.

144 Because of this it's worth checking out which artificial harmonics come out cleanly with which pick-ups.

145 You can get a note to sustain on an electric guitar for a very long time by making the guitar feedback—you'll have to be fairly loud. Just point the instrument at the amp.

146 For extra drama try ending the feedback-sustained notes with a whammy-bar dive.

Rhythm

147 One of the most important steps you can take to improve your sense of rhythm is to get a metronome. The next step is to learn how to use it. I have some sort of drum pattern click going for most of my practice time.

148 To begin with you should aim to hit the note with the beat of the metronome. However, after a while you'll realize that there are many different ways to place the beat.

149 Try the same line at the same tempo but this time try to place the note very precisely on the beat. If another part of the band is playing slightly behind the beat, this kind of rhythmic delivery can be really powerful.

150 Of course if it's your solo. you're much freer to do what you want, but if you're just accompanying then you'd do well to try to lock in with the other players.

151 Some of the 'play-along' records (backing tracks which allow you to solo over a rhythm section; such as, Music Sales' *JamTrax* series) make it possible for you to experience playing with musicians without needing to leave your house.

152 There is a downside to this approach. Once you've started to be able to play along with recordings. it's time to get out there and find some other people to play with. It's much more fun to play in a band than just be a bedroom guitarist.

All About Scales

If you have problems finding the notes which fit a particular chord type you need some help. Here's a list of some of the basic scales and the types of chords they are naturally associated with. (We have given as an example chords based on C.)

153 The C major scale—naturally associated with C major chord, C6, and C major 7th.

154 The C natural minor scale—associated with Cm7.

155 The C harmonic minor scale—used with Cm(maj7), G7♭9.

156 The C melodic minor scale. This scale can be used with Cm or Cm(maj7).

157 The C Dorian scale (Dorian mode)—very strongly associated with Cm7.

158 The C Phrygian scale (Phrygian mode). This scale is often credited with a Spanish color.

159 The C Lydian scale (Lydian mode) fits the Cmaj7♯11.

160 The Lydian flat-seven scale is perfect for the C7♯11 chord.

161 The C Lydian augmented scale. This scale fits Cmaj7+.

162 The C Mixolydian scale (Mixolydian mode)—naturally associated with the C7 chord and its extensions (C9, C13, etc.)

163 The C Locrian scale (Locrian mode). The scale is commonly used on the II of a II-V-I in a minor key. (i.e. Cm7 in Cm7-F7-B♭).

164 The C blues scale. This scale with the minor third and ♯11th, has a very characteristic sound. If the scale is new to you, be sparing in its use until you're more familiar with its color. C blues scales may be used with C major, Cm, Cm7, or C7 and various of its extensions including the C7♯9.

165 The C major pentatonic scale. All the notes in this scale are good against C major.

166 The C minor pentatonic scale.

167 The C jazz dominant scale (the 'bebop scale'). This scale was designed to fit over the C7 and Gm7 chords. The major 7th is used as a passing note to fill the gap between the root and flattened 7th degrees of the chord.

168 C whole tone scale. This scale fits C7#11.

169 The C diminished scale (often called 'half-step/ whole-step diminished'). This scale forms the basis for a wealth of great musical lines. It's probably most popular with jazz musicians. Use this scale over C7 but listen to the altered notes of the scale.

170 The C altered scale. This scale fits C7 altered (i.e. C7#9, C7#9/#5, C7♭9, C7♭9/#5, etc.). Note the similarity of this scale to the whole tone scale.

171 The chromatic scale.

Selected Chord Voicings
Major 7 Chord Voicings

172 Cmaj7

(stacked in thirds)

(taking third away from root and putting it on top of the chord)

173 Cmaj7

(moving each note up
to the nearest chord tone)

174 Cmaj7

(moving each note up to
the nearest chord tone)

175 Cmaj7

(moving each note to
the nearest chord tone)

176 Cmaj7

(taking the third and fifth and
moving them up to the next octave)

177 Cmaj7

(moving each note to
the nearest chord tone)

178 Cmaj7

(moving each note to
the nearest chord tone)

179 Cmaj7

(moving each note to
the nearest chord tone)

Dominant 7 Chord Voicings

180 C7

(taking the third away from the root
and putting it on top of the chord)

181 C7

(moving each note to
the nearest chord tone)

182 C7

(moving each note to
the nearest chord tone)

183 C7

(moving each note to
the nearest chord tone)

184 C7

(taking the third and the fifth and
moving them up to the next octave)

185 C7

(moving each note to
the nearest chord tone)

186 C7

(moving each note to
the nearest chord tone)

187 C7

(moving each note to
the nearest chord tone)

Minor 7 Chord Voicings

188 Cm7

(taking the away from the root
and putting it on top of the chord)

189 Cm7

(moving each note to
the nearest chord tone)

190 Cm7

(moving each note to
the nearest chord tone)

191 Cm7

(moving each note to
the nearest chord tone)

192 Cm7

(taking the third and the fifth and
moving them up to the next octave)

193 Cm7

(moving each note to
the nearest chord tone)

194 Cm7

(moving each note to
the nearest chord tone)

195 Cm7

(moving each note to
the nearest chord tone)

Expanding the Basic Chords

196 When you see a basic C major chord you can add the 6th or 9th to give a slightly different edge to the sound.

197 To make a major chord brighter you can try adding the 9th degree of the scale on top. (C becomes Cadd9). The Police often used this chord (check out 'Every Breath You Take').

198 In songs where there is lot of time spent on the tonic 7th chord, you might try a 7♯9 chord. Check it will fit in with the melody. This is a funky/bluesy kind of sound.

199 In heavy metal style songs you may even find yourself slimming the chords down to the bare root and fifth, at least for some part of rockier tunes.

200 In funk tunes where a minor 7th type chord is held for a long period try alternating between the minor 7th and minor 6th. This sounds best if you keep the minor 7th to minor 6th movement on the top line of your voicing. Check out some James Brown records.

201 If there's a dominant seventh (a V7 chord) you can precede it with a minor 7th chord a fifth higher. This makes a II-V progression and can add a little more movement to a chord progression.

202 As always you need to keep your ears open to I decide whether the chords fit in with the style of music you I playing,

203 If you have this:

you could play:

204 Or you could play:

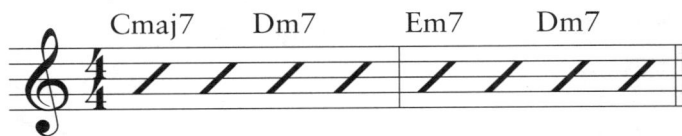

205 If a chord moves to another a fifth below you can often make the first chord a dominant 7th. For:

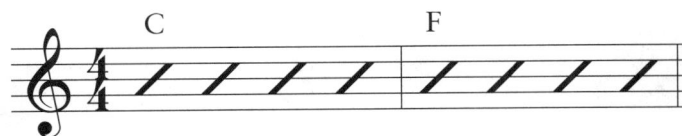

you could play:

206 For:

you could play:

207 For the last example remember that the C7 chord will sound best with a flat 13th (A♭) as this notes signals we're going to Fm *not* F major.

208 The same rule can apply to the II-V progression. For:

you could play:

Thus we're taking advantage of the fact that the Cm moves down a fifth to slot in as a dominant 7th resolving temporarily on F7, which in turn would resolve to B♭. This device is called a *secondary dominant*.

209 Jazz musicians often use altered dominant 7ths. For:

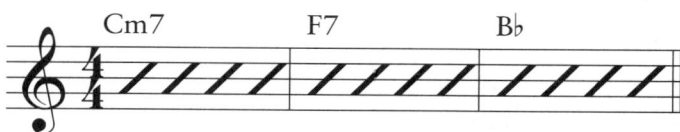

you could play:

or:

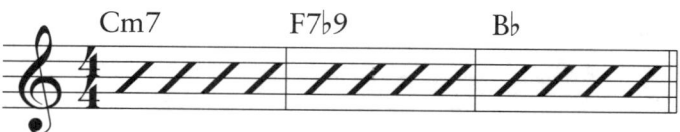

Other altered extensions you could try are the sharp 11th (raised 4th degree), the flat 13th or even the 7th with added 11th degree.

210 Normally when the 11th is present in a 7th chord the third is omitted.

211 For:

you could play:

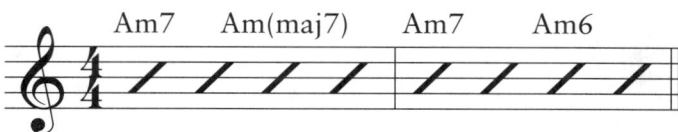

212 While we're talking jazz, it's often possible (melody permitting) to use a dominant 7th with sharp 9th for the tonic chord. Jazz pianist Bill Evans plays this type of chord at the opening of the beautiful standard 'When I Fall In Love'. This is also a favorite Jimi Hendrix sound (check out 'Purple Haze').

Learning to Listen

213 The ability to discern intervals and chords directly relates to the speed at which you will pick up new music.

214 Don't get discouraged if you find it difficult hearing what's going on in a piece of music. A large amount of pitch recognition is to do with familiarity.

215 Be patient—when you can recognize the interval between two notes in a melody, the next step is to find the interval between the next two. Pretty soon you'll be hearing the connection between larger groups of notes. Have faith.

216 Practice the following exercises when you're going about your daily business—walking down the road, lying in the bath, etc., etc.

In the Bleak Mid Winter (minor 2nd)

217 Alouette (major 2nd)

218 Oh Susanna (minor 3rd)

minor 3rd

219 Humpty Dumpty (major 3rd)

major 3rd

220 The Eensy Weensy Spider (perfect 4th)

perfect 4th

221 Maria (West Side Story)(augmented 4th)

augmented 4th

222 Twinkle, Twinkle Little Star (perfect 5th)

perfect 5th

223 Old King Cole (minor 6th)

minor 6th

224 My Bonnie Lies Over the Ocean (major 6th)

major 6th

225 Somewhere (West Side Story) (minor 7th)

minor 7th

226 Over the Rainbow (major 7th)

major 7th low E♭ to D

227 Over the Rainbow (octave)

octave

Riffs Section

Rock and Rhythm

228

229

230

231

232

233

234

235

236

E

237

G

238

Gadd2

239 Harmonics

use delay

240

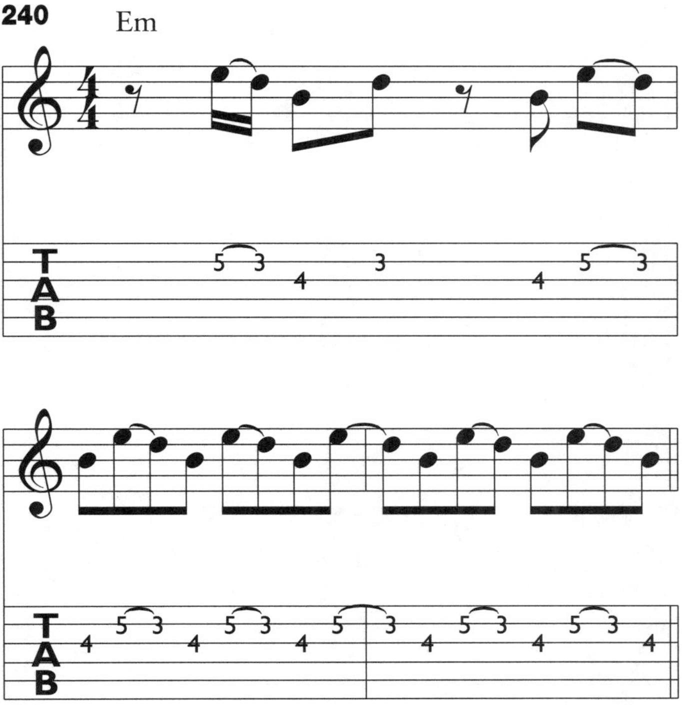

241

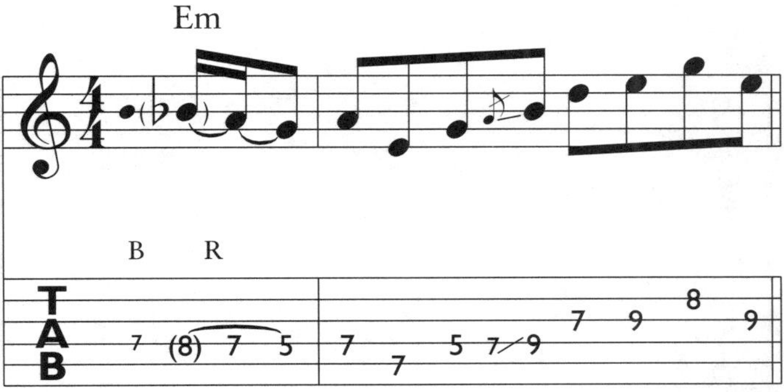

242

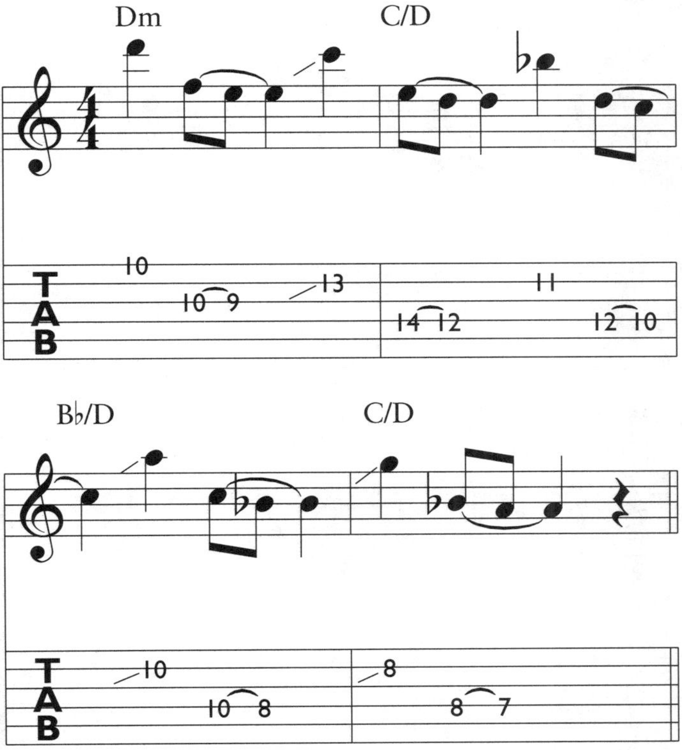

243

244

245

246

247

248

249

Blues Riffs

250

251

252

Blues Turnarounds

253 Last two bars of an E blues.

254 Last two bars of an E blues.

255

256

257

258

259

260

Blues Guitar Licks

261

262

263

264

265

266

267

268

269

Blues Scales in Open Tunings

270 Open E blues scale tuning.
Tune guitar to E B E G♯ B E

271 Open D blues scale tuning.
Tune guitar to D A D F♯ A D

272 Open G tuning.
Tune guitar to D G D G B D

Slide Guitar

Some Ideas in Standard Tuning

273

274 Try to execute the slide down to the open string cleanly.

Country Guitar

275

276

277

278

279

280

Funky Rhythms

281

282 Soul Groove

283 Reggae

284 Palm muting

Jazz Chords

285

286

287 When presented with this melody:

you could try playing it in a chordal manner:

288 Add in some other moving notes

289 Now add an altered note E♭ (♭13 on G7)

290 If you're playing in a setting where there's no other chordal instrument it's useful to be able to hit chords while playing a melody or solo
Try this:

291 If you're accompanying a singer on a Latin tune (not a swing tune) you could try this kind of accompaniment.

Jazz Walking Bass

♫ = ♩³♪ throughout this section.

292 Notes marked with * are chromatic passing notes, i.e. they are not found in the scale.

293

Gm7　　　　C7　　　　F6

294

Gm7　　　　C7　　　　F6

295 These basslines always sound much more solid
when the root of the chord is played on the first
beat of the bar. To this end, you may often need
to slip in chromatic passing notes. These are
notes which are not found in the scales used but
fill in the gap between two scale notes.
You'll probably notice that placing at least some
of the chords on the offbeat sounds a bit more
jazzy.

Gm7　　　　　　C7

F6　　　　　　　　Fmaj7

Jazz Solo Ideas

♩♩ = ♩ ³ ♩ throughout this section.

296

297

298

299

Gmaj7 Am7 D7 (G)

(using the G blues scale)

300